Grandmother's

Precious Moments™

Grandmother's
Precious Moments™

Illustrations by **Samuel J. Butcher**

Text by Gwendolyn and Steve Hines

Markings

from Thomas Nelson, Inc.

Published in Nashville, Tennessee, by Thomas Nelson Inc., Publishers

Printed in the United States of America

ISBN: 0-8407-2355-5

To
My Precious
Grandchild

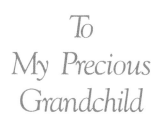

_____

From

_____

_____
Date

Precious
Beginnings

Family Tree

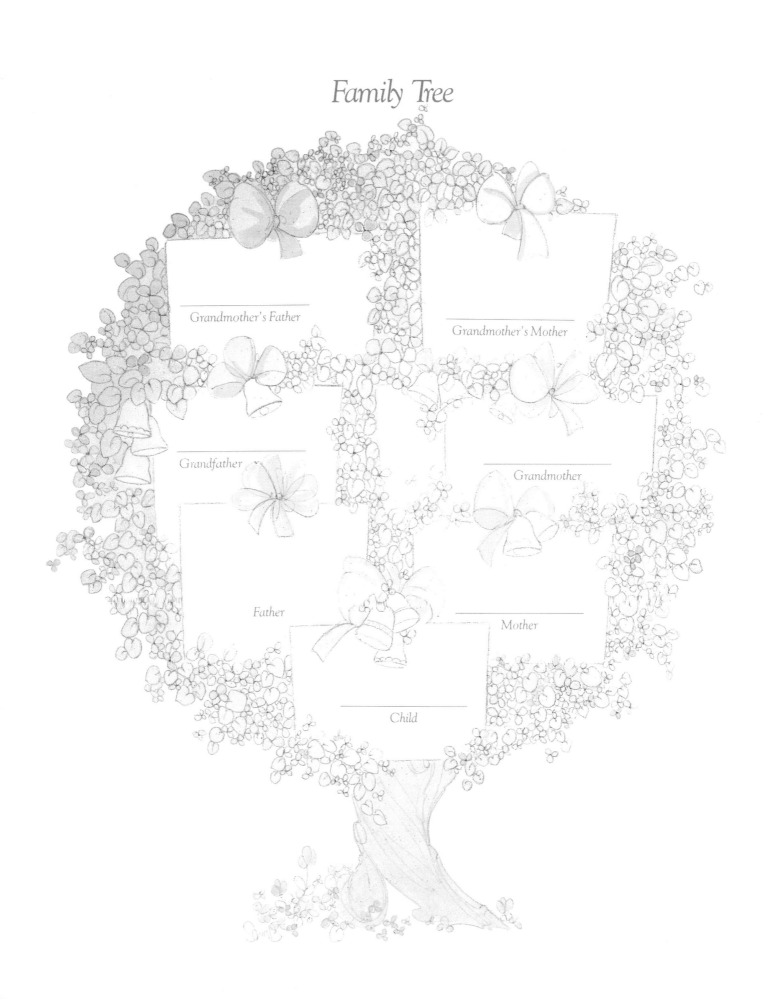

Grandmother's Father

Grandmother's Mother

Grandfather

Grandmother

Father

Mother

Child

My Birth

I was born on _____
date and time

At _____
hospital or home

In _____
city, state or county

To _____ and _____
father   mother

The story of my birth

_____

_____

_____

_____

_____

My parents said I was early to _____
walk, talk, etc.

I was late to _____

They said as a baby I _____

_____

_____

My favorite nursery rhyme, lullaby, first stories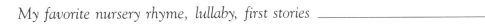

_____

_____

_____

My Childhood

Special friends _____

_____

_____

_____

Favorite dolls and toys_____

_____

_____

Favorite books _____

_____

_____

Something special that belonged to me _____

_____

_____

What school was like _____

_____

_____

_____

A special childhood memory _____

_____

_____

I remember as a teenager _____

_____

_____

What I remember best about my parents _____

_____

_____

_____

Romance

I remember during my courting days _____

_____

I met your grandfather _____

_____

_____

And we were engaged _____

_____

_____

My Husband

His parents' names

_____

_____

His birth and childhood

_____

_____

_____

_____

_____

What attracted me to him

_____

_____

_____

His work

_____

_____

_____

Our Marriage

When _____

date and time

Where _____

_____

I wore _____

_____

_____

What I remember best about my wedding day

_____

_____

_____

Our honeymoon

_____

_____

_____

A special memory or two from our years of marriage

My Precious Children

Your Parent's Birth

My child was born on _____
date and time

At _____
home or hospital

In _____
city, state or county

We lived at _____

_____

I remember especially about that day _____

_____

_____

_____

Weight _____

Height _____

Hair color _____

Your parent as a baby was _____

_____

_____

_____

I kept as a keepsake:

My Children

Names, birthdates, special memories of other children in my family

_____

_____

_____

_____

_____

_____

_____

_____

_____

_____

_____

_____

_____

_____

_____

_____

_____

_____

Your Parent's Childhood

Memories I have of your parent:

As a toddler _____

_____

_____

_____

_____

As a 4- and 5-year-old child _____

_____

_____

_____

_____

_____

_____

_____

_____

_____

_____

_____

School Days

Schools your parent attended _____
_____
_____
_____

Friends _____
_____
_____
_____

Favorite subjects _____

_____

_____

_____

Grades _____

_____

_____

We were especially proud when _____

_____

_____

_____

Something your parent did that I saved

Your Parent's
Teenage Years

Fads of the time _____
_____
_____

My child liked to _____
_____
_____

Favorite music, books, sports, movies, heroes _____
_____
_____

Your parent was especially good at _____
_____

Your parent belonged to or participated in _____
_____
_____

Your parent rebelled or made mischief when _____
_____
_____
_____

First date _____

_____

_____

Signs of growing responsibility _____

_____

_____

A graduation memory _____

_____

The Family
Grew Up Together

Vacations _____

_____

_____

_____

_____

_____

_____

The family worked together at _____

_____

_____

_____

Your parent helped out by _____

_____

_____

A favorite family story

Precious Moments
Day by Day

Home Sweet Home

My childhood home _____
_____
_____
_____

What I loved best about my home _____
_____
_____

When we visited my grandparents' home _____
_____
_____
_____

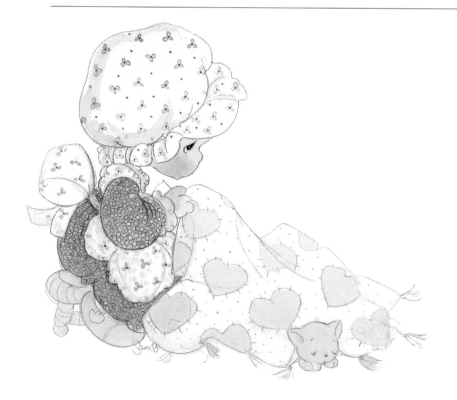

Pets

As a child _____

_____

_____

As an adult _____

_____

_____

A memory of a special pet _____

_____

_____

Hobbies

Hobbies as a child _____

_____

_____

Hobbies as an adult _____

_____

_____

A hobby that won recognition _____

_____

Entertainment

Favorite radio programs _____
_____
_____

Favorite movies, movie stars _____
_____
_____

Favorite television shows _____
_____
_____

Favorite musical styles, composers, performers _____
_____
_____

Favorite books, authors _____
_____
_____
_____
_____
_____
_____

Creative Interests

Painting, drawing, writing, composing, dancing, acting, playing an instrument, singing, etc.:

Done as a child _____

_____

_____

_____

Done as an adult _____

_____

_____

Favorite art, artists _____

_____

_____

Games

Board games, ball games, group activities, jump rope rhymes, doll play, playing school, etc.:

That I remember as a child _____

_____

_____

_____

That I enjoy as an adult _____

_____

_____

_____

Sports

Sports I've enjoyed as a participant:

Group sports _____

_____

Individual sports _____

_____

Sports I've enjoyed as a spectator _____

_____

My favorite team _____

_____

My favorite athlete _____

Fashions

A childhood outfit I especially remember _____
_____
_____

Fashion fads I wore _____
_____

My favorite style _____
_____

A special article of clothing I made or purchased _____
_____
_____

Your parent looked best in _____

My Family Church

My childhood churches _____

_____

_____

Our family church _____

_____

_____

My own milestones in church life:
(baptism, christening, dedication, confirmation, conversion, church membership, church camp, etc.)

_____

_____

_____

I remember when your parent _____

_____

_____

Special pastors, spiritual leaders _____

_____

Special friends at church _____

_____

_____

_____

My responsibilities in the church _____

_____

_____

My favorite hymn/psalm/song _____

_____

My favorite Bible passage _____

_____

Precious Moments That Make Memories

Favorite
Holiday Memories

New Years _____

_____

_____

Valentine's Day _____

_____

_____

Easter _____

_____

_____

Mother's Day _____

_____

_____

Fourth of July _____

_____

_____

Memorial Day/Veteran's Day _____

_____

_____

Halloween _____

_____

_____

Thanksgiving Memories

Thanksgiving customs _____
_____
_____
_____

A special Thanksgiving memory _____
_____
_____
_____

Things I am especially thankful for

Christmas Memories

Special Christmas customs _____

_____

_____

_____

A special Christmas memory _____

_____

_____

A favorite gift I received _____

_____

A special memory of your parent at Christmas _____

_____

_____

Favorite Holiday
Foods and Decorations

As a child _____

_____

_____

As an adult _____

_____

_____

Your parent's favorite holiday foods _____

_____

_____

_____

_____

I remember when your parent made _____

_____

_____

I remember helping to make _____

_____

_____

Special Recipes to Share

Favorite Family Stories

About my parents and grandparents _____

_____

_____

_____

_____

About my aunts, uncles and cousins _____

_____

_____

About my brothers and sisters and their children _____

_____

_____

About my husband and his family _____

_____

_____

_____

About me _____

_____

_____

About my children _____

_____

_____

Precious Moments
With The Family

Special Family Times

A special birthday I had _____
_____
_____
_____

A special birthday for your parent _____
_____
_____
_____

Anniversaries

Helping my parents celebrate _____
_____
_____
_____

Our special anniversaries _____
_____
_____
_____
_____

A special party _____

_____

_____

A birthday or anniversary surprise _____

_____

_____

The Seasons

Spring memories

Summer memories

Fall memories

Winter memories

Family Mementoes

Favorite gifts received as a child _____

_____

_____

Favorite gifts received as an adult _____

_____

_____

A special gift I gave to you _____

_____

A special gift you gave to me _____

_____

Some family heirlooms

Favorites

My favorite:

House _____

Car _____

Hand-me-down _____

Season _____

Travel destination _____

Jewelry _____

Item from bygone days _____

Invention during my lifetime _____

Others

Your Parents

Their meeting _____

_____

_____

Their wedding day _____

_____

_____

_____

A special memory of the two of them

Your Precious Birth

Where I was _____

_____

_____

My thoughts at your birth _____

_____

_____

What you mean to me and the family

_____

_____

_____

Who you remind me of _____

A special memory of you

A Grandmother's
Message to You